BEFORE DISCLOSURE
DISPELLING THE FOG OF SPECULATION

A PRIMER FOR STUDENTS OF
UFOLOGY AND EXOPOLITICS

Gerard Aartsen

Before Disclosure – Dispelling the Fog of Speculation
A Primer for Students of Ufology and Exopolitics
First published October 2016. Revised April 2017.

Copyright © 2016 Gerard Aartsen, Amsterdam, the Netherlands.

The moral right of the author has been asserted.

Photo credits:
Page 18: Pablo Dessy. Page 21: Alberto Perego. Page 34: Vladimir Voychuk. Page 35: Iyaxin.com.

ISBN-13/EAN-13: 978-90-815495-6-1

Published by BGA Publications, Amsterdam, the Netherlands
www.bgapublications.nl

Typeset in Calisto MT and Calibri

Cover photograph: A luminous golden UFO appears in a photograph of the aurora borealis taken by Ingrid Kristin Johnson Lanan in Andoya, Norway on 22 October 2015. According to information coming from Benjamin Creme (Share International magazine, December 2015), this is a spacecraft which usually works underground on Earth.

Contents

Introduction

As highly speculative accounts of possible doom from space began to take precedence in the 1960s, the accounts of the original contactees were being derided and dismissed, and increasingly they were portrayed as mystics who were trying to peddle some new kind of religion to the gullible.

Except, when one actually reads their accounts, it is astounding to see how much of their information chimes not only with the Golden Rule as a central notion in all the world's religions and humanity's own highest aspirations as enshrined, for instance, in the Universal Declaration of Human Rights, but also with the current social and economic situation in the world, the crises facing humanity, and the latest scientific insights.

While corporate interests are attempting to tighten their grip on governments and policies to secure their power and wealth, disclosure of any kind at this time would have to be met with the same suspicion of a hidden agenda as the initial cover-ups of extraterrestrial visits and the subsequent disinformation campaign.

As a result of widespread disinformation, these days UFO researchers and enthusiasts are not just faced with derision among the general public and the mainstream media, but with rampant speculation about the extraterrestrial presence from within their own ranks as well.

Therefore, the essays in this volume are intended to help the reader distinguish between corroborated facts and speculation, as well as remove the need of many today to find an 'alien' scapegoat, or saviour, as the case may be, for the dire situation that we ourselves, as a planetary species, have created and need to resolve.

About the author

Gerard Aartsen (1957) is an author, speaker, researcher and educator from Amsterdam, the Netherlands. He earned his Master of Education degree from the Amsterdam University of Applied Sciences where he has held a teaching position at the department of secondary education since 2001. He has also been a lifelong student of the Ageless Wisdom teaching and is the author of several books on the subject of the extraterrestrial presence. His books have been translated and published in various languages and his articles have appeared in magazines around the world. The author is a frequent guest on international radio shows about UFOs and related subjects, and has lectured about his work in America, Europe and Asia.

For more information: www.bgapublications.nl.

1. Untangling facts from disinformation

With speculation in the field of Ufology and exopolitics increasing exponentially by the year, or so it seems, and the craft visiting from outer space making their presence felt more visibly by the day, let us not waste any time acknowledging the proverbial elephant (or mothership) in the room: If the modern world was unaware of the space visitors and their intentions before the 1950s contactees began to write and speak about their experiences, why are researchers today ignoring their information and do we allow our perception to be obscured by the disinformation that was meant to discredit them?

Take, for example, the story that recently did the rounds on the internet (again) that at least four out of "82 alien species are fighting for control over Earth"[1], based on videos that are supposed to present the findings of 'researchers'.

Anyone with a passing knowledge of the history of the extraterrestrial presence on Earth would immediately wonder why it should take them so long to 'take control', given that apparently they possess the technology to cover vast distances through space to come here, and that – based on ancient records of their presence – they have been coming here for centuries, if not millennia. Also, since most people do not even take the extraterrestrial presence seriously, we might share in renowned astrophysicist Carl Sagan's wonderment why more of the neighbours wouldn't have noticed?[2]

What's more, if we go back to the spate of contacts that inaugurated the modern age of Ufology in the early 1950s, the one outstanding fact is that none of the contactees, whose accounts were not contaminated by the disinformation campaign, had anything but positive experiences to share. The message they

1

were asked to convey, even if just a few short years after the end of World War II and under the palpable threat of nuclear war, was one of empowerment for the human race: We must avoid further armed conflict if we are to prevent self-annihilation, and it is feasible to create a peaceful future through international co-operation and making sure everyone's basic needs are met, as an expression of the oneness of humanity.

However, being engaged in a nuclear and conventional arms race with the Soviet Union, the Western industrial-military complex, which includes the fossil and nuclear fuel industry, felt this message was not in their interest. So much so, that governments and their military who needed the public's support for their ideological warfare and global arms race, decided in the mid-1950s that, despite the cover-up of the army's salvaging of one or more crashed flying saucers, the contactees' message of international co-operation for peace and brotherhood was being too well received. An indication of this popularity can be found in the fact that, within three years of its publication *Flying Saucers Have Landed* (1953), the book which included George Adamski's initial contact experience, was reprinted twelve times in the US alone and published in seven (!) other languages.

Because attempts to silence these harbingers of a different, saner way of life with offers of money or intimidation did not bring the desired effects, it was decided to discredit their experiences and defame their character. At the same time, film makers were enlisted to seed confusion in the public mind with features such as *Invaders from Mars* (1953), *Earth vs the Flying Saucers* (1956), *Invasion of the Saucer Men* (1957), et cetera. So obvious was this effort that *Flying Saucer Review* eventually published a 'Special Editorial' in its issue of March-April 1959 stating: "We abhor this trend to condition world opinion through films and other media to fear the space ships."[3]

Meanwhile, secretive government agencies were set up to

stage scary experiences ("military abductions" or MILABS, cattle mutilations, et cetera) in order to engender fear of the visitors from space.[4] It is significant to note here that the first reported case of alleged 'abduction' by beings from space, which involved a couple named Betty and Barney Hill, did not occur until 1961. Why would 'they' have waited for their first 'abduction' until after the notion of an 'alien threat' had been introduced into the public perception?

In light of the above, we should be very careful about embracing any information involving extraterrestrial visitors or technology that reaches us via 'government insiders' or 'whistle blowers' who may or may not have worked at secret laboratories, for the simple fact that we can never be certain whether their information wasn't deliberately planted to feed or increase the public's fear and confusion.

Many of the 'secret space programme' (SSP) claims, for instance, coming from 'whistle blowers', seem to rest on a statement allegedly made by the late Lockheed Skunk Works engineer Ben Rich: "We now have the technology to take ET home." But military aviation historian Peter Merlin, who attended many of his talks, explains that this statement was merely misconstrued from a successful tagline which Mr Rich used at the end of his talks since 1983: "The Skunk Works has been assigned the task of getting [the movie character] E.T. back home."[5]

Given these circumstances, claims of 'secret space programmes' that involve humanity's power elite roaming the solar system with the help of "off-world allies" cannot be scrutinized for accuracy, and are only corroborated by fellow 'whistleblowers' whose backgrounds are equally unclear and whose sources cannot be scrutinized either. Besides, who had heard of 'secret space programmes' before Ronald Reagan's ill-conceived Strategic Defence Initiative of 1983, or even before the fictional governments of Earth decided to co-operate for a planetary defence system in the *Independence Day* blockbuster of 1996?

Corroboration across disciplines

EXAMPLE 1: THE SPACE VISITORS' INTENTIONS:

"If [the UFOs over nuclear weapons bases] wanted to destroy them, with all the powers they seem to have, they could have done that job. So I personally don't think that it was a hostile intent."
—Robert Salas, US Air Force Captain, Ret. (2010)

"It is complete nonsense that [the space people] should carry out genetic or sexual experimentation on people from this planet when they have a technology which is several thousand years ahead of anything that we could think of today."
—Benjamin Creme, esotericist (2010)

"[T]hey do not abduct people; this phenomenon that today gets so large an echo in UFO books cannot be charged to them."
—Bruno Sammaciccia, contactee (2009)

"It's pretty obvious that if [the ET presence] had been hostile we would have been gone by now. (...) We have no defence, if that is what their real intent was."
—Edgar Mitchell, astronaut (2008)

"Why should beings so advanced in physics and engineering – crossing vast interstellar distances – be so backward when it comes to biology?"
—Carl Sagan, astronomer (1993)

"We all know the power [the space people] have tapped would make our largest bombs look like dud firecrackers on the 4th of July. Do not these facts adequately answer questions regarding their hostility?"
—George Adamski, contactee (1957)

In contrast, we do have assurances, again via the first contactees, that the visitors "would gladly give you this knowledge [of overcoming gravity] which has served us so well, except that you have not yet learned to live with one another in peace and brotherhood, for the welfare of all men alike, as we have on other worlds. If we revealed this power to you or to any Earth man and it became public knowledge, some of your people would quickly build ships for space traveling, mount guns upon them and go on a shooting spree in an attempt to conquer and take possession of other worlds."[6] We need to ask ourselves, therefore, if peaceful visitors did bother to explain why they wouldn't share their technology with us just yet, why would they not have warned us about their competitors from space, if indeed such a threat existed?

There is no doubt that since Nazi Germany powers have been working in secret to develop space faring technology. Yet that doesn't prove anyone actually managed to develop a craft that has been able to take us beyond the moon. Desmond Leslie, who has been nearly forgotten as the first to give an overview of the history of extraterrestrial visitations in his part of the book *Flying Saucers Have Landed*, provided a most compelling argument in this respect. He subtly remarked that "the only objection to the 'Alien [i.e. enemy] Power Theory' is that these saucers have been flying all over the world (of friend and foe alike) for rather a long time. Researches show that they appeared in large numbers and were seen by eminent astronomers years before the Wright Brothers had made their first successful heavier-than-air flight. In that case, any earthly power which had them in its possession must be of a very peaceable nature, for it could have conquered the world, practically overnight, any time it so chose."[7] Clearly, as natural resources are becoming scarcer, this applies even more today than it did in 1955.

And as recently as 2008, the late Apollo 14 astronaut Dr Edgar Mitchell, who said of himself that he was "privileged enough to be in on the fact that we have been visited on this planet" and not just anyone to say so, asserted in an interview: "I suspect that in the last 60 years or so there has been some backengineering (...) but it is not nearly as sophisticated yet as what the apparent visitors have."[8]

Hence, we can see how claims of 'secret space programmes' result from speculation gone out of orbit – breakaway imagination, more than the 'breakaway civilization' that some speculate about. For those who want to arm themselves against the infectious fear-driven narrative it is hoped the above considerations will show readers *how* to think, not *what* to think.

It should be clear that the alleged atrocities that many currently ascribe to 'aliens' only entered the discourse about extraterrestrial contact some time after the campaign to ignite confusion and fear for the space visitors was launched, much like we had never heard of the 'Blue Avian' species[9] before the film *Avatar* (2009) became a huge hit with cinema-goers. Clearly, the disinformation campaign has not only wrought havoc in people's trust of the 'official' story but also in their critical faculties, so that many now see conspiracies even where there are none – or lose sight of reality. So much so, that the alarmists and fantasists now seem to outnumber those who make a genuine effort to separate fact from fiction. Time, therefore, to bring back logic and common sense to our efforts.

As many would agree, 'truth' is a matter of perception, but a person's perception very much depends on their stage in conscious evolution. For instance, when Carl Sagan stated in his famous TV series *Cosmos*: "We're made of star stuff. We are a way for the cosmos to know itself", what he said was no different than when Jesus said "I and the Father are One", as an expression of his identification with the Source of all life. This, in turn, is no different than when George Adamski wrote in 1958: "[Man must] understand that he is one with **all creation**. He must comprehend that the atoms vibrating in his present body have been used and reused throughout creation; therefore, they have participated in every phase, from the lowest conceivable form, to immense planetary bodies that ages ago were absorbed back into space. There are no divisions except those man has imposed upon himself!"[10]

So we see how statements such as Sagan's astrophysical assertion, which was expressed more prosaically by George Adamski, whom many would consider a layman, are merely another way of expressing what others see as a doctrinal part of the Christian religion. Therefore, while 'truth' may differ from one person to the next, depending on their conscious development, if an experience is of universal value it will be recognized and confirmed from different angles, regardless of the particular department of human endeavour in which the person expressing it is active. We could call that cross-discipline corroboration – science and religion, in this case, expressing the same truth from their respective experience of reality.

According to Benjamin Creme, whose work is considered by many as the latest exponent of the Ageless Wisdom teaching, "God is an experience to be expressed. You expand your consciousness to become aware. It is all to do with awareness."[11] In much the same vein Peter Harrison, Director of the Institute for Advanced Studies in the Humanities at the University of Queensland, Australia, recently said that "the starting point for both science and religion is some form of experience, and the point is to make sense of that experience."[12]

Now, because secrecy and cover-ups have spawned seemingly unlimited speculation about the nature of the extraterrestrial presence on Earth, even among those who consider themselves researchers, we need to establish a way to ascertain which information, facts, experiences, or claims deserve our earnest attention and which we can safely discard. Knowing that the disinformation campaign was meant to destroy the reputation of the first contactees, so that they would no longer be taken seriously, their accounts provide a reliable starting point, especially since they all exhibit many striking correspondences. More so because they find confirmation not only from contactees in other parts of the world at that time, but also from many who have reported similar experiences in later decades. These correspondences, which I have documented extensively in my books, include respect for our free will and our right to self-determination as a species, but also concern about the way we have organised society around the destructive need to compete for a living.

Obviously, there are also contradictions or dichotomies in contactees' reports, but these never relate to the main aspects of the nature of their contacts or the intentions of the visitors, and may be due to reasons ranging from a limited perception; a lack of understanding; distortion in the information conveyed due to either of the former or life-long conditioning; the need for fictionalization; or fear of ridicule – all on the part of the contactee. Such discrepancies, however, are for these very reasons of far less importance than statements that not only mutually support each other, but confirm the tenets of humanity's shared wisdom traditions as well.

As I explained in *Priorities for a Planet in Transition*, by looking for correspondences with regard to crucial characteristics through qualitative research, and synthesising our findings, we can deduce a valuable set of criteria – historical, social, political and spiritual – which may serve as touchstones for scrutinizing essentially any claim regarding the extraterrestrial presence. To summarize, if we were being visited by both benevolent and malevolent extraterrestrials...

- there is no reason why contact of only one type should have occurred without that of the other type happening during the time of the first reported contacts;
- there is no reason why malevolent contact at any time would

not have been reported by officials and dignitaries, several of whom *have* reported benevolent contact;

- we should also have reports of contacts promoting the opposite of international co-operation, justice, and peace, as well as offers of further destructive technology, through some of the original contactees;
- we should have reports of life philosophies or teachings from some early contactees that not only coincide with or confirm the basic teachings of humanity's shared wisdom traditions and religions, but with opposing teachings or views on life as well.

If we now apply these criteria to the prolific claims of 'abduction', we will quickly see that such do not stand up to the critical synthesis of our qualitative data or, indeed, logic. For, if abduction by visitors from space was an authentic phenomenon, should there not have been one among the many people in the 1950s around the world who came forward with their stories of contact? Likewise, should there not also have been an official or dignitary among those who have spoken out about contact with people from space, to say they had experienced being abducted?

To be sure, this is not to deny anyone the experience they have had. As I indicated in the explication of the research method I use for my work, there are at least four plausible explanations for 'abduction' experiences: (1) when people adopt the prevailing terminology – 'abduction' – for what is basically a consensual contact experience, even if the strangeness of the memories induced feelings of fear (e.g. Travis Walton no longer refers to his contact experience as an 'abduction' but as "an ambulance call")[13]; (2) when secretive government or military agencies stage a hypnosis- or drug-induced experience intended to confuse and mislead the public about the true nature of the extraterrestrial presence; or when sensitive people either (3) have an overactive imagination, or (4) tap into the thoughtform that has built up around this phenomenon, and convince themselves it happened to them, just as dreams are real at the time of the dreaming.[14]

Thus, in order to decide if information can be trusted to reflect some level of truth or reality beyond strictly subjective experiences, we only need to see if it finds confirmation from several angles, or at least more than one, from people across time, disciplines and/ or social strata. This is essential in a field like Ufology, because tangible proof will be impossible until the time of open contact. After all, as a result of the disinformation campaign that has been going on for decades, even 'disclosure' by governments or their agencies will have to be subject to doubt simply because they depend on public support for their (geo) political agendas.

Readers will note that our approach, therefore, is not a case of looking for confirmation of set beliefs to the exclusion of contradictory evidence, but rather a tool to eliminate disinformation, misinformation, and speculation. In this regard, corroboration from a religious teaching is just as valuable as that from a scientific source.

It should be remembered here that science, or a scientific approach, does not equal atheism. To wit, evolutionary biologist Richard Dawkins' atheism is itself a belief, and no less fundamentalist than that which sees the Bible as taken down verbatim from the mouth of God, rather than a collection of 66 books that make up the two Testaments, written by many prophets, priests and scribes or their followers over many generations. It is precisely this type of rigid extremist thinking that invariably leads to conflict, whether in the religious, the scientific, the political or the economic field – with tolerance, respect and right human relations as its inevitable and ultimate victims.

Anyone who cares to study humanity's shared wisdom traditions will find that the essence of religions – the original teachings minus the dogma that subsequent interpreters (priests) allowed to accrue around them – shares several crucial points of agreement, most important among them: (1) the cyclical revelation through the return of a Teacher, at the beginning or end of each cosmic cycle or Age, about (2) the source and evolution of consciousness, which needs to be given expression by (3) living according to the Golden Rule to establish right human relations.

Many may find comfort in dismissing religion for the rigid dogma that later interpreters formed around the original teaching that informed it, and who falsely claimed they were meant as a one-off immovable Divine directive, but that is about as short-sighted as dismissing claims of contact because of the ridicule that was bestowed on the accounts of the original contactees by the powers-that-be. However, an unbiased look at both the original teachings and the original accounts of contact with extraterrestrial visitors shows they are pointers to a way of life based on growth of consciousness through right human relations.

Indeed, anyone who has read the accounts of the first contactees will know that the extraterrestrial visitors – although their counsel and teaching may have been cloaked in the 'religious sounding' terms with which these contactees were familiar – had nothing to do with religion in the sense of 'deferring responsibility' to an external authority, but on the contrary, invariably called on our own responsibility to right the wrongs in our world, as documented extensively in *Priorities for a Planet in Transition*.

Again, when we go along with unbridled speculation that, for instance, religions might be thought manipulation by the visitors from space, we are not contributing any form of clarity but merely muddying the waters with a less obvious type of fear. And it is fear and ignorance that have led humanity astray from the essence of the Teachings into the dogma and extremism that have created the dangerous divisions of the present day.

The definition of science that Daniel Fry's contact gave him during their encounter in July 1950 provides a tantalizing bridge between our current understanding of science and religion,

11

as "the orderly, and intelligently directed, search for truth" divided in three principal branches: (1) the physical or material science, which deals with the relationship between man and his physical surroundings; (2) the social sciences, which describe the relationship between man and his fellow man; and (3) the spiritual science, which covers the relationship "between man and the great creative power and infinite intelligence which pervades and controls all nature".[15]

That this 'bridge' is not necessarily wishful thinking on my part is confirmed in a 2012 comment by professor of Physics Stephen M. Barr at the University of Delaware, USA, who wrote that if we "accept the more traditional understanding of quantum mechanics that goes back to Von Neumann, one is led by its logic (...) to the conclusion that not everything is just matter in motion, and that in particular there is something about the human mind that transcends matter and its laws. It then becomes possible to take seriously certain questions that materialism had ruled out of court: If the human mind transcends matter to some extent, could there not exist minds that transcend the physical universe altogether? And might there not even exist an ultimate Mind?"[16]

Professor Barr is far from the only scientist who has arrived at this or a similar notion about the ultimate nature of Reality. What's more, as Daniel Fry's contact from space explains: "Mankind (...) no matter where or when he may come into being, is endowed with the innate realization that there is an infinite intelligence and a supreme power which is greater than man's ability to comprehend. During the many stages of his development, man's attitude toward this power may vary from fear and resentment, to reverence and love. But he has always had the instinctive desire to learn more of the spiritual side of his nature and the creative sphere of this power."[17]

Likewise, one of George Adamski's contacts elaborated: "We of other worlds who have been living unrecognized amongst you can see clearly how identity with Divine origin has been lost. People of Earth have become separate entities which are no longer truly human in expression as in the beginning they were. Now they are but slaves of habit. Nonetheless, imprisoned within these habits is still the original soul that yearns for expression according to its Divine inheritance. (…) [U]ntil man can cast off the shackles of his personal self-pride and allow this voice to guide him, he will continue to live as a warrior against the laws of his own being."[18]

As shown in *Priorities for a Planet in Transition*, the accounts of the first contactees of the modern age of UFOs are brimmed with information and advice for us to build a new world that will ensure the survival of the race and the safe progress of its civilization. Based on the body of evidence in that book, and its pertinence to the state of the world today, I suggested a more practical and evidence-based definition of the term 'exopolitics', which goes back to the original meaning of its constituents, with 'exo' meaning "(from) outside" and 'politics' meaning "matters concerning the state or its citizens":

Exopolitics – People from other planets showing humanity alternative, saner ways of organising society, without imposing their views.

As the facts which we can safely identify from looking at the history of modern contact with extraterrestrial visitors are ignored, it is no wonder that the story of the six blind men who try to identify an elephant by the one part of its body that happens to be in front of them, is a most apt allegory for the present state of research into UFOs and the extraterrestrial presence.

However, in an environment governed by secrecy and disinformation we must approach the subject of – and evidence for – extraterrestrial visitations with our eyes open to the full picture, while maintaining a critical attitude towards any claims of contact or 'insider' knowledge that have come forward since the start of the disinformation campaign.

The only way we can do this is by acknowledging the many striking similarities in the accounts of the first contactees in the wider context of the human experience, and taking these as a touchstone against which to scrutinize any claims that may be at risk of contamination from the fear, confusion and sensationalist attention-seeking that has exceedingly characterized most of the contact narrative from the mid-1950s onward.

Round-up

Basic facts

- Invariably, the contactees of the 1950s reported being contacted by benevolent people from space who pointed out the dangers of socio-economic inequality in a divided world with nuclear weapons at our fingertips, and the need for international cooperation to solve humanity's problems for our survival and the safe progress of our civilization.
- The notion of visitors from other planets and the positive message coming from contactees such as George Adamski, Daniel Fry, Buck Nelson, Howard Menger, and many others triggered massive interest from a war-weary public living under the psychological threat of nuclear annihilation.
- Because of the ideological stand-off between the West and the East Bloc during the Cold War, the powers-that-be needed the public's support for their arms race and started a concerted disinformation campaign, designed to discredit the contactees' experiences and ridicule their information and their character.
- The greater the number of different social, academic and religious backgrounds among those whose experiences are compared, the more reliable and valid the findings of this qualitative research proves to be.

Implications

- Doubt, confusion and fear resulting from deliberate disinformation and scare tactics such as staged 'abductions', opened the doors to rampant speculation among the public as well as less-than-discerning researchers.

Corroborations

- The state of the world today confirms the urgent need for international cooperation, socio-economic justice and peace, as advocated by the visitors from space in the writings of the original contactees.
- The evident higher morals and ethics of the space visitors has already been

recognized in humanity's highest aspirations, such as the Universal Declaration of Human Rights and the conclusions and recommendations in the 1980 report by the Independent Committee on International Development Issues (aka the Brandt Commission), *North-South – A Programme or Survival.*

- The information about the benign intentions of the visitors from space from the original contactees finds corroboration in the accounts of later contactees from around the world, as well as in accounts of officials and dignitaries.
- The notion of the Brotherhood of Man that the space visitors pointed out to the original contactees can also be found in the Golden Rule, which we find at the heart of every religion on Earth, as well as in the Ageless Wisdom teaching.
- Increasingly, scientists and followers of religion find common ground in acknowledging the reality of a transcendent power beyond the observable universe.

Notes

1 Johnthomas Didymus (2016), 'UFO Researchers: 82 Alien Species Are Currently in Contact With Earth – And At Least Four Are Fighting For Control over Earth'. *Inquisitr* (online), 19 August. [Accessed 24 August 2016]

2 Carl Sagan (1983), 'Are they coming for us?' *Parade* magazine, March 7.

3 Special Editorial, 'Why This Horror From Space Trend?'. *Flying Saucer Review*, Vol.5, No.2, March-April 1959, p.15

4 See e.g. Steven Greer (2006), 'Exopolitics or Xenopolitics' (PDF).

5 Peter R. Merlin (2013), 'Taking ET home: The birth of a modern myth'. *SUNlite*, Vol.5, No.6, November-December, pp.17-19. (PDF) [Accessed 11 September 2016]

6 George Adamski (1955), *Inside the Space Ships*, p.90

7 Desmond Leslie (1955), 'Astronomy and Space-Men', *Flying Saucer Review*, Vol.1, No.3, July-August, p.23

8 Interview with Dr Edgar Mitchell in Nick Margerrison (2008), *The Night Before*, Kerrang! Radio, UK, 23 July.

9 The earliest mention of 'Blue Avians' appears in a *Stillness in the Storm* blog dated 2 March 2015. [Accessed 4 September 2016]

10 George Adamski (1958), *Telepathy: The Cosmic or Universal Language*, Part II, p.26

11 Benjamin Creme (2016), 'Questions and answers'. *Share International* magazine, Vol.35, No.6, July/August, p.35

12 Peter Harrison (2016), reply to reader's comment on his essay 'Are Science and Religion in Conflict?' *Big Questions Online*, 28 June. [Accessed 27 August 2016]

13 'Travis Walton shares new theory on Fire in the Sky alien abduction'. Open Minds TV, 2 July 2012

14 Gerard Aartsen (2015), *Priorities for a Planet in Transition*, pp.172-74

15 Daniel Fry (1954), *[A Report By Alan] To Men of Earth*, in Fry (1966), *The White Sands Incident*, pp.75-76

16 Stephen M. Barr (2012), 'Does Quantum Physics Make It Easier to Believe in God?'. *Big Questions Online*, 10 July. [Accessed 27 August 2016]

17 Fry (1954), op cit, pp.77-78

18 Adamski (1955), op cit, pp.116-17

2. Uncloaking the material reality of the UFOs

One of the enduring 'mysteries' surrounding UFOs concerns their apparent ability to appear and disappear at will. Here, too, enlightening clues can be found in the accounts of contactees and the wisdom teachings, while scientific insights continue to provide interesting corroborations.

When the first measurements of the surface temperature on Venus came in in 1958, George Adamski was quickly ridiculed for his assertion that his contacts hailed from that and other planets in our solar system. He was not alone, though, in maintaining his claims: Brazilian physicist-contactee Dino Kraspedon (pseudonym for Aladíno Felíx), Canadian researcher-contactee Wilbert Smith, Italian journalist-contactee Bruno Ghibaudi, and US contactees Howard Menger and Buck Nelson all said, more or less publicly, that the spacecraft and their occupants originate from within the solar system, mainly from Mars, Venus, Saturn and a few other planets.

While since the character assassination on the first contactees hardly anyone has placed the origins of the visitors from space within our own solar system, to this day esotericist Benjamin Creme states categorically: "All the planets of our system are inhabited..." but, he adds, "if you were to go to Mars or Venus you would see nobody because they are in physical bodies of etheric matter."[1] This underscores what contactee Howard Menger was told in the 1950s: "[I]f an Earth man in physical body could go there he probably would not see some of the life forms which vibrate more rapidly than his own – no more than he can see the spiritual life forms in and around his own planet. Unless his physical body were processed and conditioned, he could not see the beings on another planet."[2] Reversing the same notion, George Adamski also said that the space people "can place their mind in a high frequency state that causes their body to become invisible to our limited range of vision."[3] He was told, in fact, that "...we can increase the frequency of the activated area of a ship to the point of producing invisibility. Except for our own precaution, your planes could fly blindly into our ship without seeing it. If we permitted you to come as close as that, when you hit, you would find our craft as solid as though functioning in a lower frequency."[4]

Understanding the concept of the etheric (subtle) planes of matter is crucial in this respect. As the latest exponent of the Ageless Wisdom teaching Mr Creme says that, "[u]nless one understands the reality of the etheric levels of energy as finer, subtler, levels of matter, one cannot begin to understand the UFO phenomenon..."[5] However, the principle of space craft becoming visible by lowering the rate of vibration of their atoms, or disappearing from our sight when they return to their original state, is really not very difficult to understand when his space contact explains to Chilean contactee Enrique Barrios: "If a bicycle wheel turns rapidly, you can't see the spokes. We make the molecules of the ship move rapidly."[6]

That the same principle applies to the occupants of the craft is implied in an episode from Truman Bethurum's book *Aboard a Flying Saucer*. When Truman and his boss Whitey are having coffee and pie at a local diner, they notice a woman whom Tru recognizes as the captain of the flying saucer that he met before, with one of her crew members. His boss doesn't want to be introduced and goes to wait outside, and Tru asks him to watch which way the space people go when they leave the restaurant. When Tru asks the woman some questions she denies, but later, through the waitress, confirms that she was indeed the captain. After they leave the diner, Truman asks Whitey which way they went, but Whitey says no one left the restaurant.[7]

In a report about a close encounter with visitors from space in a wilderness reserve near Uitenhage in Eastern Cape, South Africa, on 2 October 1978, four young eyewitnesses describe to UFO researcher Cynthia Hind how they witnessed men "wearing silver suits" disappear before their eyes. When asked where these men went the boys replied: "[T]hey just suddenly disappeared", at the same time noticing that their craft "was also gone".[8]

Even though he was aware of the different levels of solid physical and etheric physical matter, George Adamski declined to make that distinction because his experiences and his message were in danger of being obfuscated by mystics who claimed they were

Space people seen in the etheric in stills from a video taken in the Cordoba province of Argentina, in 2006, where Mónica Coll filmed some of her companions on a hiking trip in the Ongamira region, north-east of the capital Buenos Aires, from a slightly elevated position at a short distance. The human figures of light were not visible to the people present at the time of filming, but were only seen in the recording afterwards. (Source: Pablo Dessy (2009), '¿Seres de luz en Ongamira?')

channelling "messages from space". However, it was precisely Adamski's mission to show the world that they are real, physical (albeit etheric physical) beings. He once told his one-time co-author Desmond Leslie: "They are not goddam spooks".[9] On other occasions, according to researcher Timothy Good, he would bolster his argument by asking: "Why would a spook need a spaceship?"[10] Many of the space people who come to Earth to help us are, in fact, highly evolved beings – as can be concluded from Adamski's description in his 1955 book *Inside the Space Ships* – who can travel anywhere by thought. However, according to Benjamin Creme, in order to help us in all the various ways that they do, they need the technology of their space ships. In fact, Mr Creme says, "Many of the large ships (they can be up

An extraterrestrial pilot photographed in Italy in 1957: "We see in fact a man with glasses, his mouth rather small, with a metal collar that is joined to a space suit of flexible and shiny fabric. We notice mysterious bracelets (...) and a mysterious device on the belly..."

Photo taken from the 1963 book *L'aviazione di altri pianeti opera tra noi : rapporto agli italiani: 1943-1963* by Alberto Perego. As a career diplomat, he would not likely risk his career by publishing photographs with a dodgy provenance. In fact, Mr Perego was a participant in the well-known Italian Amicizia Case (see page 29).

to four miles long) are mother ships, laboratories and so on."[11]

When Adamski was on a Saturnian mothership, he was told: "This ship is a scientific laboratory. We travel space solely for the purpose of studying the constant changes within space itself. We observe the life and conditions on the many planets we encounter as we move through space. (...) It is through the research made by ships like ours that space travel has been developed to the present degree of safety."[12]

As Italian contactee Giorgio Dibitonto, writing about his experiences in 1980, was informed: "The universe contains boundless regions beyond the material one that you know. The only dimension that is observed by your science is the material. (...) In the cosmos there is not only the material dimension. There are ultra-material dimensions that encompass not only length, breadth and depth, but a much greater richness of life-realities, as a consequence of which all of that which you call behind, in front of, over, under, within and without, become outmoded concepts. The higher a universe is, the more its life-force expresses itself in new, free forms, and the consciousness extends itself to a more comprehensive point of view."[13]

In his book *From Outer Space to You* Howard Menger describes how he witnessed a saucer drop into our range of vision: "The ship took the form of a pulsating, fluorescent light, changing in colors from white to green to red. As it neared I prepared to take more pictures. It came in slowly, at about the speed of a Piper Cub. When it was within a foot of the ground and about a hundred feet from the car, it hovered, and I recognized the familiar bell shape. The pulsating colors stopped, it gave off an eery, bluish light, and then portholes appeared."[14]

As mentioned above, the existence of planes of matter above the three that our current science recognizes is not new to students of the Ageless Wisdom teaching. According to these teachings, there are four levels of physical or subtle matter above the solid, liquid and gaseous – known as the etheric physical planes of matter, which consist of sub-atomic particles at various frequencies, comparable to the molecules of ice, water and vapour vibrating at different frequencies. The Tibetan Master of Wisdom Djwhal Khul has said that the etheric "is the true form to which all physical bodies in every kingdom of nature conform" and that "life itself, the training to be given in the future, the conclusions of science and a new mode of civilisation will all increasingly be focussed on this unique substance".[15] Several trailblazing scientists have also made discoveries which all seem to point to some aspect or other of the etheric planes of matter.

For instance, Semyon Kirlian's technology to record the energy fields surrounding living entities was later further developed to photograph human auras. And, in his article 'The Discovery of the Orgone', the Austrian doctor Wilhelm Reich quotes the German biologist Kammerer, who said that "the existence of a specific life force seems highly probable to me! That is, an energy which is neither heat, electricity, magnetism, kinetic energy (...) nor a combination of any or all of them, but an energy which specifically belongs only to those processes that we call 'life'. That does not mean that this energy is restricted to those natural bodies which we call 'living beings'..." Through experiments Reich subsequently established that the orgone radiation, as he called this primordial life force, permeates everything.[16]

Dense physical forms may be seen as the precipitation of the 'blueprints' that exist on the etheric physical levels, which is no longer an entirely esoteric notion since British biologist Rupert Sheldrake posited the idea of "morphogenetic fields" – a sort of memory bank from which Nature retrieves its various solid physical forms.[17] This should also make it easier to understand that Life is not solely dependent on carbon-based dense physical forms for its expression, but can also express itself in etheric physical forms, as indeed it does on the other planets in our solar system, according to the Teachings and the accounts of several contactees.

The fact that the craft of the visitors from space are in etheric physical matter precludes the possibility that anyone is abducted for gene harvesting, hybrid breeding, implanting devices, and other atrocities that the scare-mongering crowd accuses the visitors of. In fact, Benjamin Creme says: "Nobody is ever taken up in a spaceship in a physical body. It is impossible. These spaceships are not solid physical. To be taken up into a spaceship you have to be taken out of the dense physical body and you go in the etheric into the spaceship, which are in themselves etheric. It is still physical, but etheric physical."[18]

Interestingly, a possible description of the process of being taken out of the (dense physical) body also comes from Howard Menger, who describes what happened when he was finally allowed to board a ship: "[A] second man stepped outside and raised his arm. In his hand was some sort of instrument which he pointed at me. Suddenly a bluish beam shot out at me, and as it struck my head I felt a tingling sensation, warm, and rather pleasant. I stood in my tracks as he slowly played the beam downward over my body until it had reached my feet. Then he turned it off, and my friend threw up his arm, indicating that I walk ahead of him. The other man had stepped into the craft and now beckoned me."[19] His hosts later explained: "We projected the beam on you to condition and process your body quickly so you could enter the craft. What actually happened was that the beam changed your body frequency to equal that of the craft."[20]

The accounts of various contactees present tacit evidence of their having been taken out of the physical body as they testified to a heightened state of awareness once they were on a ship. Giorgio Dibitonto, for instance, writes: "The light within this wonderful ray-ship produced an effect on us which I was unable to explain. We felt freshened and renewed, and all our spiritual energies rejoiced in an indescribable sense of peace. At the same time, we found ourselves in a state of well-being which changed us and awakened all the sleeping powers within us. We felt keenly receptive to all that might be imparted to us by words and images. Our hearts burnt with an all-inclusive love, such as is rarely felt on Earth."[21]

The American contactee Orfeo Angelucci, too, seems to give some impression of what it must feel like once one is in this 'unearthly' state: "The interior was made of an ethereal mother-of-pearl stuff, irridescent [sic] with exquisite colors that gave off light… There was a reclining chair directly across from the entrance. It was made of the same translucent, shimmering substance – a stuff so evanescent that it didn't appear to be material reality as we know it… As I sat down I marveled at the texture of the material. Seated therein, I felt suspended in air, for the substance of that chair molded itself to fit every surface or movement of my body. As I leaned back and relaxed, that feeling of peace and well-being intensified."[22]

The similarities of Angelucci's descriptions with those of other contactees are striking. For instance, Dibitonto writes: "The central room was illuminated with light that seemed to come from all directions, as no single light source was to be seen. … An unaccustomed empathy prevailed; we were all flooded with this same unearthly light, and with an energy that was more spiritual than physical."[23] Likewise, Howard Menger noted: "[T]he walls became brighter, as if illumined somehow from inside themselves…"[24]

George Adamski described the interior of a disk as follows: "Within the craft there was not a single dark corner. I could not make out where the light was coming from. It seemed to permeate every cavity and corner with a soft pleasing glow. There is no way of describing that light exactly. It was not white, nor was it blue, nor was it exactly any other color that I could name."[25]

Scientist Michael Wolf's description of the interior of a saucer is strongly reminiscent of Adamski, Angelucci and Dibitonto's descriptions: "We were standing in what seemed to me as a very familiar room, brilliantly lit, but not as much as to hurt the eyes. The light seemed not to emanate from any single source, but was everywhere. The doorway that closed appeared not to have any juncture or architectural connection or seams or handle."[26]

Meanwhile, mainstream science is still grappling with this expanded view of reality, even though Swiss astronomer Fritz Zwicky already proposed 'dark matter' in the 1930s as a working hypothesis for the 96 per cent of the known universe that science cannot account for, but which astrophysical calculations of the mass of the universe predict.

In March 2015 the 'avant garde' scientific ideas pursued or proposed by Kirlian, Reich and Sheldrake, which all point in the same direction as (partial) explanations for 'dark matter' or 'dark energy', almost stealthily gained confirmation when mainstream science published findings, as reported in *The Independent* newspaper, which "suggest that dark matter is another kind of sub-atomic particle, possibly forming a parallel universe of 'supersymmetry' filled with supersymmetrical matter that behaves like an invisible mirror-image of ordinary matter."[27] This in turn is reminiscent of what Howard Menger was told: "Nothing we see with our physical eyes is Truth, but simply a reality in the dimension of a reflection, or an effect, secondary in nature related to a Cause from a primary Source."[28]

Commenting on the recent discovery of traces of micro-organisms dating back 3.7 billion years, also in *The Independent*, Dr Abigail Allwood, of Nasa's Jet Propulsion Laboratory provided a scientific underpinning for the notion that 'life' is not quite as unique as previously thought: "Earth's surface 3.7 billion years ago was a tumultuous place, bombarded by asteroids and still in its formative stages. If life could find a foothold here, and leave such an imprint that vestiges exist even though only a minuscule sliver of metamorphic rock is all that remains from that time, then life is not a fussy, reluctant and unlikely thing. Give life half an opportunity and it'll run with it. (…) Suddenly, Mars may look even more promising than before as a potential abode for past life."[29]

With this acknowledgement of the abundance of life, and the expanded view of life that presents itself in the corroborations presented here, when we next read scientific assertions that there is no life on the other planets in our solar system, we would do well to add "…on the dense physical planes of matter".

This essay is expanded from an article which was first published in **Share International** *magazine, Vol.35, No.3, April 2016, with adaptations appearing in* **UFOlogist Magazine** *(Australia),* **UFO Truth Magazine** *(UK) and* **Paranormal Underground Magazine** *(USA).*

Round-up

Basic facts
- Space craft are able to appear and disappear at will, and change their appearance ranging from translucent or balls of light of various colours to solid physical craft.
- Based on astrophysical calculations about its mass, mainstream science cannot account for 96 per cent of the known Universe, which it has labelled 'dark matter' and 'dark energy'.
- Esoteric wisdom teachings have always posited the notion of etheric (ie subtle) planes of matter above the dense, liquid and gaseous physical, on which sub-atomic particles vibrate at a higher frequency than on the planes below it.

Implications
- There exist states of matter that are currently unknown to mainstream science.
- Space craft can move out of and into their original state, which lies outside our current range of vision.
- Statements coming from the early contactees point to their out-of-body experiences, i.e. experiences in the etheric counterpart of their physical bodies.
- Other planets in our solar system are inhabited although Life there does not – or no longer – precipitate onto the dense physical planes of existence.

Corroborations
- 'Avant-garde' scientists in various fields have provided evidence for the likelihood of

the existence of invisible (etheric) planes of matter.

- The latest insights of mainstream science as to the nature of 'dark matter' and the proliferation of 'life' seem to point to precisely such invisble planes of subtle matter.
- Since the first cases of contact were reported, contactees the world over have spoken about their contacts from planets within our solar system, although their relentless defamation through the disinformation campaign of the 1950s seems to have pushed many – contactees as well as perhaps contacts – to refrain from such identification of their origins.

Notes

1   Benjamin Creme (2001), *The Great Approach – New Light and Life for Humanity*, p.129
2   Howard Menger (1959), *From Outer Space to You*, p.162
3   George Adamski (1965), *Answers to Questions Most Frequently Asked About the Space Visitors and Life on Other Planets*, p.16
4   Adamski (1955), *Inside the Space Ships*, p.156
5   Creme (2010), *The Gathering of the Forces of Light – UFOs and their Spiritual Mission*, p.67
6   Enrique Barrios (1989), *Ami, Child of the Stars*, p.42
7   Truman Bethurum (1954), *Aboard a Flying Saucer*, pp.91-94
8   Cynthia Hind (1982), *UFOs – African Encounters*, pp.138-143
9   Desmond Leslie and George Adamski (1970), *Flying Saucers Have Landed*, Revised and Enlarged edition, p.250
10 Timothy Good (1998), *Alien Base – Earth's Encounters with Extraterrestrials*, p.152
11 Creme (2001), op cit, p.133
12 Adamski (1955), op cit, p.135-36
13 Giorgio Dibitonto (1990), *Angels in Starships*, p.42
14 Menger (1959), op cit, p.74
15 Alice A. Bailey (1950), *Telepathy and the Etheric Vehicle*, p.139
16 Wilhelm Reich (1960), *Selected Writings*, p.195
17 Rupert Sheldrake (1981), *A New Science of Life – The Hypothesis of Formative Causation*
18 Creme (2010), op cit, p.49
19 Menger (1959), op cit, p.83
20 Ibid, p.84
21 Dibitonto (1990), op cit., p.82
22 Orfeo Angelucci (1955), *The Secret of the Saucers*, pp.20-21
23 Dibitonto (1990), op cit, p.6
24 Menger (1959), op cit, p.83
25 Adamski (1955), op cit, p.50
26 Michael Wolf (1996), *The Catchers of Heaven*, p.199
27 Steve Connor (2015), 'The galaxy collisions that shed light on unseen parallel Universe'. *The Independent* (online), 26 March. [Accessed 27 March 2015]
28 Menger (1959), op cit, p.173
29 Ian Johnston (2016), 'World's oldest fossils found in discovery with "staggering" implications for the search for extraterrestrial life'. *The Independent* (online), 31 August. [Accessed 2 September 2016]

3. Uncovering the mission of the space people

As we saw in the previous chapter, while we cannot presently look to mainstream science for confirmation of the reality of extraterrestrials visiting Earth, we can use its findings to look for corroborations of claims of contact that stand up to scrutiny as outlined in chapter 1.

The Swiss scientific magazine *Life* recently reported that, given adequate time and habitat, life will more likely than not evolve into complex forms wherever it occurs[1],which supports the notion of the predictability of evolutionary outcomes[2] (aka evolutionary convergence). Simply put, this means that the evolution of life, regardless where it occurs, is disposed to result in similar forms. At the opposite side of the spectrum that ranges from scientific reasoning to religious faith, Pope John XXIII seemed to provide confirmation of this notion when he said, after an encounter with a being from a space ship in the garden of his summer palace in July 1961: "The sons of God are everywhere. Sometimes we have difficulties in recognizing our own brothers."[3] In light of these corroborating statements the claims of the first contactees that they were contacted in the 1950s by human-looking beings from other planets gain a whole new significance.

The papal corroboration is further strengthened by statements to the same effect from other dignitaries and officials, such as FIDE President and former President of Kalmykia Kirsan Ilyumzhinov; Italian Consul Alberto Perego; Bulgarian professor Lachezar Filipov; Italian university professor Bruno Sammaciccia; and Italian science and aviation journalist Bruno Ghibaudi, whose direct personal experiences confirm that the human form is a universal occurrence (see page 30).

Associate professor of Philosophical Anthropology at Erasmus University Rotterdam (the Netherlands) Ger Groot recently wrote an article titled 'Would it really be so strange to speak of 'extraterrestrial brothers'?'. As if reflecting on the current state of speculation-rife UFO research, he said: "Who knows, humanity might one day look back with incomprehension at our future encounter with life from space. For, just as [when we ourselves encountered different cultures] in the 16th century, we will not immediately recognise the destiny we share with them. At first we will likely overlook these 'brothers' entirely."[4]

Being among the very first to go public with his experience, which was witnessed by six others, George Adamski gave a description in 1958 which goes a long way toward confirming professor Groot's musings: "The visitors have made themselves inconspicuous while on Earth, conforming rigidly to our customs; for they are aware many people still find it hard to believe advanced human beings surround us in space. They are cognizant of the ridicule those whom they contact must face…"[5] Likewise, Wilbert Smith, the Canadian engineer and contactee said: "In several instances reliable people have reported seeing the beings who ride about on these craft, and they say they look just like us. There are quite a number of reported contacts between these people from elsewhere and people of Earth (…) and the results of these contacts are remarkably consistent and enlightening."[6]

One of the visitors who contacted Adamski told him: "We live and work here, because, as you know, it is necessary on Earth to earn money with which to buy clothing, food, and the many things that people must have. We have lived on your planet now for several years."[7]

In order to keep a low profile, they do ask for help from their contactees sometimes, as Howard Menger elaborates: "I found I was actually helping them in little material ways… Often I purchased clothing and took it to the points of contact. Visitors just arriving from other planets had to be attired in terrestrial clothing so they could pass unnoticed among people."[8] Very similar accounts have come forward from the Italian Amiciza (Friendship) Case of contact with well over a hundred Italians, that started in 1956.[9]

Another American contactee, Buck Nelson, was also told there are many space visitors among us: "The folks I talked to spoke English very well. It seems that they learn the language of the people they will be contacting. They have told me that there are many of them amongst us. They have even taken some of our government officials up in their ships, but the officials are afraid to tell about it for they have too much to lose. I have no family to suffer for what might happen to me."[10] In blatant violation of the freedom of thought so strictly adhered to by the space visitors, and echoing the experiences of George Adamski, Bruno Ghibaudi and many others, Mr Nelson intimated: "I cannot say that I have been threatened, but I was offered a check for a thousand dollars if I would never tell my story again."

Chilean author Enrique Barrios, who wrote about his 1985 experience in his novel *Ami, Child of the Stars*, was told that contact with individuals, as has been the space visitors' modus operandi, does not constitute interference with our evolutionary development. "To show ourselves openly, to have mass communication, would be..."[11], and if there were to be a mass landing "thousands of people would die of shock. Remember all your movies about invaders? We are not inhumane, we wouldn't want to cause something like that."[12] Indeed, as I have documented in my books, the space people are acting from the advanced moral standpoint that each planet, each nation, as well as each individual, has the inalienable right to determine their own destiny, while at the same time it has been pointed out by many of the visitors from space since the 1950s that they are here to assist humanity in what appears to be a crucial stage in our evolution. Hence, the

Corroboration across disciplines and social strata

EXAMPLE 2: THE HUMAN FORM IS UNIVERSAL

"The sons of God are everywhere. Sometimes we have difficulties in recognizing our own brothers."
—Pope John XXIII

"They are people like us. They have the same mind, the same vision. I talked with them, I understand that we are not alone in this whole world [universe]. We are not unique."
—FIDE President and former President of Kalmykia Kirsan Ilyumzhinov

...the human form is "universal throughout the Cosmos, as part of a general harmony – and yet the idea of this has generally been rejected by Earthmen as impossible, no doubt, as almost always, the truth is too simple to be accepted." –Italian science and aviation journalist Bruno Ghibaudi

"The human model is universal – head, trunk and extremities – but there are small variations on each world: height, skin, color, shape of the ears, small differences."
—Enrique Barrios, Chilean author of *Ami, Child of the Stars* (based on an experience he had in 1985)

"...man is universal; you may find small variations from one race to the next, even among ourselves you have seen very tall persons (...) and very small ones; there may be differences in the skin colour, there are people whose flesh is almost transparant, but, I repeat, almost every civilization is made up of man..."
—The space visitors through Bruno Sammaciccia, Italian contactee

"Space travelers are identical to us, only they have a deeper understanding of themselves and the Cosmos of which we are all inhabitants."
—George Adamski, US contactee and author

"The human race in the form of MAN extends throughout the Universe, and is incredibly ancient..."
—Canadian engineer and contactee Wilbert Smith

"They are men, and certainly better than us because of the tolerance and patience demonstrated in the face of our atomic madness."
—Italian Consul Alberto Perego

"They are human. Indeed, in comparison it's we terrestrials who are less than human. They are much more human than we are..."
—Anonymous participant in the Amicizia Case (through Nikola Duper)

frustration of many UFO 'believers' about the visitors not showing themselves results from the fact that they are treading the thin line between non-interference and assistance in the form of protecting us from our own destructiveness. For instance, according to Italian Consul Alberto Perego in 1963, "We must be grateful to them for the permanent dredging of our atmosphere, which, without them, would have already been irreparably contaminated by residues of our atomic explosions. We must be grateful to them for having prevented, until now, nuclear war."[13]

Indeed, the visitors are not here to present humanity with a 'paranormal' phenomenon or, as Adamski assured us, "to satisfy our personal curiosity. At the present time, I have been told, the best way we can help is by beginning to live with more respect toward one another. For as this is done throughout the world, fear and hostility between the peoples will diminish; leaving a fertile field in which to work for the betterment of all."[14]

In other words, while science confirms that physical evolution anywhere is likely to follow a path similar to that which it took on Earth, the visitors from space are eager to inform us that the evolution of consciousness should not only be manifested in our technological progress, but also in our moral development. The first step in this direction is for humanity to expand its consciousness to include our fellow man, in order to eradicate the cause for the present crises, which our social structures are presently bringing to a head, based as they are on competition and greed as the ultimate expression of our separativeness. Not for nothing did Daniel Fry's contact tell him that "the needs and desires, the hopes and fears of all the people of your earth, are actually identical. When this fact becomes a part of everyone's understanding, then you will have a sound basis for the formation of the 'One World' of which your politicians speak so glibly and your spiritual leaders speak so wistfully."[15] Likewise, Adamski's contacts said to him: "If man is to live without catastrophe, he

31

must look upon his fellow being as himself, the one a reflection of the other."[16]

Science journalist John Horgan, author of *The End of Science: Facing the Limits of Knowledge in The Twilight of The Scientific Age*, recently wrote in a blog entry: "What if science boosts our minds' power without giving us greater self-understanding? Shouldn't that be cause for concern?"[17] For the space people it certainly is and it is for this reason that they implore us: "Now that your scientific knowledge has so far outstripped your social and human progress, the gap between *must* be filled with urgent haste."[18]

Many other contacts from space have indicated that our moral development is a necessary expression of the evolution of consciousness, which is itself facilitated by the evolution of the physical forms that was meticulously documented by Darwin. The world's major religions, too, refer to the evolution of consciousness. The following concise rundown can be found in a book by organizational learning pioneer Peter Senge, *Presence – Human Purpose and the Field of the Future*: In the esoteric Christian tradition the evolution of consciousness is associated with 'grace' or 'revelation'; Taoism speaks of the transformation of vital energy (qing) into subtle life force (qi) and spiritual energy (shi); Buddhists strive after 'cessation' of thought, or 'enlightenment'; in Hinduism it is referred to as 'wholeness' and in mystical Islam it is known as 'opening the heart'.[19]

Since it can be found at the heart of every major religion, we should not be surprised to see that the notion of the evolution of consciousness is indeed central to the Ageless Wisdom teaching, which states that out of the human kingdom has evolved another kingdom in nature that consists of the Masters and Initiates of Wisdom from whose midst a Teacher is sent into the world at the beginning or end of every new age or cosmic cycle.

The Master of Wisdom whom UK esotericist and contactee Benjamin Creme has been working with since 1959 indicated the limitations of both the scientific and the religious understanding of evolution in an article from 2008: "[E]volutionists and the creationists are really arguing at cross-purposes; both, in their limited way are right. (...) The creationist is at pains to emphasise that 'Man' was made by God, in 'God's own image', and so owes nothing to evolution. To such, Darwin and those who follow him are missing the point about Man: that he is a spiritual being, of divine heritage... From Our point of understanding the scientists of today, the evolutionists, are undoubtedly correct in their analysis of Man's development from the animal kingdom. (...) That, however, does not make us animals. Darwin, and those who correctly followed his thought, describes only the outer, physical development of Man, largely ignoring that we are all engaged in the development of consciousness. The human body has all but reached its completeness: there remains little further to be achieved. From the standpoint of consciousness, however, man has scarcely taken the first steps towards a flowering which will prove that man is indeed divine, a Soul in incarnation."[20]

Although the role of the contactees was simply to expand humanity's awareness with the notion that man exists throughout the universe, including the solar system, several have hinted at the actual purpose of the extraterrestrial presence at this time in human history.

As Enrique Barrios was told in 1985: "You are approaching a decisive point in Earth evolution, a time when you either unite and bring about what some call the 'Age of Aquarius', or you destroy yourselves."[21] During his contacts in 1980 the Italian contactee Giorgio Dibitonto had been given a very similar message: "[T]he people of Earth should prepare themselves for a new journey, one that has no equal in all your history. No single event that ever yet happened on Earth, can compare with that which stands before you now. ... Clouds and pillars of fire, which today you would call flying saucers and motherships, were seen over the leaders of the Hebrews who fled from Egypt. Exactly the same signs and realities portend in these days a new and final journey, which will lead you out of your present misery, into the true promised land of universal love. (...) We will accompany you ... as we did in those days, and our presence will be much more in evidence this time. (...) We will help you in every way that we can. We will be pillars of cloud by day, and pillars of fire by night."[22]

In a lecture he gave in Detroit (Michigan, USA) in September 1955 George Adamski said: "[I]t states in our own Bible that in the latter days (as we might call it at the moment) that when these things will be happening ... like 'signs in the sky and war and rumors of war' ... we will have come to an end of a cycle, or as some people call it, a 'dispensation'."[23] And: "It's not only our own earth but the whole system that is going through a change which is a cycle that is coming to an end and another will take its place."[24] In light of these statements, it seems that his insistence elsewhere that there is nothing to the 'Age of Aquarius' was

"We will be pillars of cloud by day..." (Photo of UFO clouds over Kamchatka Peninsula, taken by Vladimir Voychuk on 14 August 2015. Source: weather.com)

merely another of his attempts to keep his mission and his information from being obscured by mystic notions, much like Ufology at present has been taken over by speculative hypotheses at the expense of the information that we do have.

On various occasions George Adamski testified to the many commonalities among the various religions as different expressions of the same truth (see also page 10), among which the cyclical appearance or return of a Teacher, which he did again in answer to questions posed by a minister in the audience, at his lecture in Detroit, confirming that "there have been many messiahs…"[25] In the Wisdom teachings, in which Adamski was versed as a teenager[26], this cyclical appearance of a Teacher is known as the Doctrine of the Coming One, which is also evinced in almost every religion: Christians are waiting for the Second Coming, Jews are still expecting the Messiah, Buddhists await the fifth Buddha, Hindus the tenth incarnation of Vishnu, or Kalki Avatar, and segments of Islam are waiting for the return

"…and pillars of fire by night." (Photo of UFO seen over a wide area in the Xinjiang region of western China on 11 January 2010. Source: www.iyaxin.com)

of the twelfth Mahdi, or Imam Mahdi.

According to British author and esotericist Benjamin Creme, who gave talks about the spiritual mission of the Space Brothers in the 1950s, this time is no exception. He has been informing the world that in July 1977 the World Teacher for the new age arrived in London as his centre in the modern world and has since been preparing mankind and the world for his open manifestation at the earliest possible moment.[27]

Due to the massive speculation that now prevails in the field of Ufology, for many the concept of craft and visitors coming from outer space to support the inauguration of a new cosmic age will probably seem less plausible than 'jump rooms' from which members of humanity's 'breakaway civilization' can get to their 'secret bases' on Mars. Yet, in the context of this chapter, Benjamin Creme's statement in his first book (1979) may be seen as corroboration from the Ageless Wisdom teaching: "[W]hat we call the U.F.O.'s (the vehicles of the space people from the higher planets) have a very definite part to play in the building of a spiritual platform for the World Teacher, preparing humanity for this time."[28]

This throws a whole new light on what Wilbert Smith learned from his contacts, first published in his 1958 article 'The Philosophy of the Saucers': "In time, when certain events have transpired, and we are so oriented that we can accept these people from elsewhere, they will meet us freely on the common ground of mutual understanding and trust, and we will be able to learn from them and bring about the Golden Age all men everywhere desire deep within their hearts."[29]

Readers who feel all this confirms their suspicions about the information from the early contactees being Messianic or neo-religious messages that promise salvation so people will no longer want to think or act for themselves, might want to think again. For the books and pamphlets that these pioneers have written all show their agreement that the visitors from space can only help us if we choose to save ourselves, as one after the other exhorts humanity to take responsibility to right the wrongs in our world (and according to Benjamin Creme the same applies to the World Teacher). As George Adamski said: "Today, we again stand at a momentous crossroads. The space travelers are doing their utmost to warn and help us. But the final decision lies in our hands."[30]

Others, who are cracking their brains on a 'new paradigm' that will save us, will find that in the final analysis any new dispensation will require nothing less than humanity finally beginning to give expression to our innate oneness, by creating universal justice and freedom through the acceptance of the principle of sharing as the basis for our economic affairs.

With Dr Carl Sagan and others before him stating that we are all born of the same stardust[31], and given everything else science has come to acknowledge about the nature of life as it expresses through evolution, combined with the accounts of the early contactees, the correspondences in all the major religions, and humanity's shared Wisdom tradition, we may well ask ourselves which part of (extraterrestrial) life could justifiably be called 'alien'? For, what would it be alien to?

To be sure, when it comes to our annihilation, we seem to be managing all too well without outside help. For this reason, we would more adequately reserve the term 'alien' to indicate attitudes and behaviours that go against the universal values that – given freedom from want and fear – the human heart exhibits on Earth and elsewhere: respect, tolerance, freedom and justice for people and planet – and which are urgently needed as an expression of the next step in our conscious evolution.

The basis for this essay first appeared as a panellist contribution in **JAR** *Magazine (online), 25 August 2016.*

Round-up

Basic facts
- Several high-profile individuals testify to the reality of visitors from space coming to Earth, confirming the experiences of the first contactees of the modern age.
- Science increasingly confirms the likelihood of life existing around the universe, along the lines of predictable evolutionary outcomes.
- All major religions share the notion of the expansion of consciousness, facilitated or inspired by the cyclical revelation of a new or returned Teacher.
- The original contactees were informed that humanity's moral progress must keep in step with our technological advancement to prevent our self-destruction.

Implications
- If humanity is innately one, as testified by the visitors from space in their contacees' accounts, the essence of the world's religions and advancing scientific insights, the socio-economic inequality that divides the world today could well be seen as the manifestation of a crisis of consciousness, showing a fundamental lack of correct human relations.

Corroborations
- The Ageless Wisdom teaching posits the notion of a kingdom in nature that has evolved from the human kingdom, which consists of men and women who have evolved beyond the strictly human state – the Masters of Wisdom.
- As the most recent exponent of the Ageless Wisdom teaching, Benjamin Creme has been informing the world that the Teacher for the New Age is ready to make himself known to the world and inspire humanity to create a new civilization based on socio-economic justice and freedom for all.
- Several contactees were told that humanity is standing on the treshold of a new cosmic cycle, often referred to as the Age of Aquarius, and that the visitors from space are here in support of this transition, as they were on similar occasions in the past.

Notes

1 William Bains and Dirk Schulze-Makuch (2016), 'The (Near) Inevitability of the Evolution of Complex, Macroscopic Life'. *Life* magazine [online], Vol.6, Issue 3 (30 June). [Accessed 12 August 2016]
2 Matthew Wills (2016), 'What do aliens look like? The clue is in evolution'. *The Conversation* (online), 19 August. [Accessed 2 September 2016]
3 'Juan XXIII, el papa que habló con un extraterrestre'. *Diario Popular* [online], 27 April 2014. [Accessed 12 August 2016]
4 Ger Groot (2015), 'Is het zo gek om te spreken van een "buitenaardse broeder"?'. *Trouw* [online], 16 August. [Accessed 17 August 2015]
5 George Adamski (1957-58), *Cosmic Science for the Promotion of Cosmic Principles and*

Truth – Series No. 1, Part No. 3, Question #57

6　Wilbert Smith (1969), *The Boys from Topside*, p.21

7　Adamski (1955), *Inside the Space Ships*, pp. 38-39

8　Howard Menger (1959), *From Outer Space to You*, p.71

9　For a comprehensive history and overview of the Friendship Case, see Gerard Aartsen (2011), *Here to Help: UFOs and the Space Brothers*, Chapter 4, 'From Space in Friendship'

10　Buck Nelson (1956), *My Trip to Mars, the Moon, and Venus*, p.13

11　Enrique Barrios (1989), *Ami – Child of the Stars*, p.32

12　Ibidem, p.26

13　Alberto Perego (1963), *L'aviazione di altri pianeti opera tra noi : rapporto agli italiani*: 1943-1963, p.534

14　Adamski (1957-58), op cit, Part No.2, Question #25

15　Daniel Fry (1954), *[A Report By Alan] To Men of Earth*, in Fry (1966), *The White Sands Incident*, p.91

16　Adamski (1955), op cit, p.239

17　John Horgan (2016), 'The Mind-Body Problem, Scientific Regress and "Woo" '. *Scientific American* Cross Check [online], 11 July. [Accessed 7 September 2016]

18　Adamski (1955), op cit, p.137

19　Peter Senge et al (2004), *Presence – Human Purpose and the Field of the Future*, p.14

20　Benjamin Creme's Master (2008), 'Evolution versus creationism'. *Share International* magazine, Vol.27, No.10, December, p.3

21　Barrios (1989), op cit, pp.99-100

22　Giorgio Dibitonto (1990), *Angels in Starships*, pp.32-33

23　Adamski (1956), *World of Tomorrow*, p.1

24　Ibid., p.4

25　Ibid., p.13

26　Aartsen (2010), *George Adamski – A Herald for the Space Brothers*, pp.22-23

27　Creme (ed.), *Share International* magazine, Background information

28　Creme (1979), *The Reappearance of the Christ and the Masters of Wisdom*, p.206

29　Wilbert Smith (1958), 'The Philosophy of the Saucers'. *Flying Saucer Review*, Vol.4, No.3, May-June, p.11

30　Adamski (1957-58), op cit, Part No.3, Question #49

31　Garson O'Tool (2013), 'We Are Made of Star-Stuff'. *Quote Investigator* [online], 22 June.

The extraterrestrial presence and the evolution of consciousness – the connection in 6 steps

1. Life is not the result of a chemical 'accident' due to favourable conditions in some parts of the Universe, but the underlying Cause of the eternal, cyclical evolution and expression of consciousness, as it manifests itself as the Universe.
2. Likewise, consciousness is not the outcome of a chemical reaction in the human brain but the 'vehicle' through which Life expresses and experiences itself on every level – be it a galaxy, a solar system, a planet, a human being, or an atom.
3. All who, through the evolution of consciousness, have attained a greater measure of awareness – i.e. all the great historical Teachers of humanity, the Avatars of the East, as well as visitors from space – hold before us the same view of universal, interconnected Life and evolving consciousness.
4. They also teach us that, being universal, Life is One, and intricately interconnected throughout the Universe, and therefore that life on planet Earth is One. Ignorance or negligence of this fact always creates adverse conditions for humanity to the point of self-destruction.
5. Although the global elites are doing everything to prevent humanity from giving expression to this awareness – as this would undermine their economic and financial power which they yield through systems based on greed and competition – in this historical time of planetary transition we see that more and more members of the human race are beginning to respond to the notion that Life is One and that humanity is One.
6. The accounts of the first contactees of the modern era abound with advice on how to give expression to the awareness that we are One human family, by creating a society based on justice and freedom to ensure the survival of the human race and the safe progress of its civilization.

Life is One, the world is One, humanity is One.

RECOMMENDED READING

Beyond speculation and sensationalism, the author brings together a significant body of information about the alternative, saner ways of organising society that space visitors have shown us since the 1950s.

BGA Publications, first edition 2015
Paperback, 212 (xii + 200) pages; incl. colour photographs and Index
ISBN: 978-90-815495-4-7

RECOMMENDED READING

HERE TO HELP: UFOs AND THE SPACE BROTHERS

GERARD AARTSEN

Message from space:
Life is One, so live as one
.... or perish

Based on extensive research, this book reframes the debate
about the intentions of the space visitors in view of
the unprecedented changes engulfing the world today.

BGA Publications, second edition 2012
Paperback, 200 (xii + 187) pages; incl. colour photographs and Index
ISBN: 978-90-815495-3-0

RECOMMENDED READING

For the first time, this book reveals the true scope of
George Adamski's mission in preparation
for a complete restructuring of our world.

BGA Publications, second edition 2011
Paperback, 158 (xii + 145) pages; incl. photographs and Index
ISBN: 978-90-8154-952-3

RECOMMENDED READING

Books by other authors:

George Adamski, *Inside the Space Ships*

Enrique Barrios, *Ami – Child of the Stars*

Benjamin Creme, *The Ageless Wisdom Teaching –
An Introduction to Humanity's Spiritual Legacy*

Benjamin Creme, *The Gathering of the Forces of Light –
UFOs and Their Spiritual Mission*

Stefan Denaerde, *Operation Survival Earth*

Desmond Leslie and George Adamski, *Flying Saucers Have
Landed*

Wilbert B. Smith, *The Boys from Topside*